Name

....

Home Address

....

....

....

Date Begun

....

Fix-It and *Don't* Forget-It™

A Cook's Journal

Phyllis Pellman Good

Illustrated by Cheryl Benner

Good Books

Intercourse, PA 17534
800/762-7171
www.GoodBooks.com

Design by Cliff Snyder

FIX-IT AND DONT FORGET-IT
Copyright ©2008 by Good Books, Intercourse, PA 17534
International Standard Book Number: 978-1-56148-631-1
Library of Congress Catalog Card Number: 2007049931

Library of Congress Cataloging-in-Publication Data

Good, Phyllis Pellman
  Fix-it and don't forget-it : a cook's journal / Phyllis Pellman Good ; illustrations by
Cheryl Benner.
     p. cm.
  ISBN 978-1-56148-631-1 (wire-o bound : alk. paper) 1. Cookery--Miscellanea. I.
Title. II. Title: Fix-it & don't forget-it.
  TX652.G66154 2008
  641.5--dc22   2007049931

Table of Contents

Use This Book!

F ix-It and <u>Don't</u> Forget-It: A Cook's Journal is one happy solution to 3 problems that every cook faces—

1. Where is that recipe I want to make?
2. What did I serve these guests the last time they were here?
3. I don't have buttermilk in the fridge. What can I substitute?

Fix-It and <u>Don't</u> Forget-It is divided into 3 handy sections to help you keep easy track of 3 things—your elusive recipes, your favorite menus, and your helpful tips.

No more chasing through cookbooks, piles, and files to find your beloved recipe for tiramisu. Use "Where Is That Recipe?" (pages 5-70) as your personal index to your scattered recipe collection. Here is the place to record the names of your favorite recipes, and the cookbooks and pages where you can find them.

Wondering what menu to serve when it's your turn to host your family or neighbors? Fearful that you'll duplicate

the dishes you made the last time the soccer team came for supper? Turn to "Food I've Served to Family and Friends" (pages 71-144), where you can record what you served (and where those recipes are found), to whom, and on what date. You'll love this organized diary of the great meals you've made.

Stuck in the kitchen without your cooking guru? Flip to "Tips to Remember" (pages 145-155) for a list of basic cooking hints and information. And there are lots of pages where you can add your own tips and important cooking know-how.

May *Fix-It and Don't Forget-It* become your kitchen companion!

Wishing you much cooking convenience and pleasure,

Where is That Recipe?

I love recipes. That means I'm constantly tearing them out of magazines and putting them on my "try-as-soon-as-possible" pile. I pick up a new cookbook and mark the "gotta-try-soon" recipes. The cookbook gets a prime spot in the kitchen. I prepare a great recipe and add it to my "make-it-again" pile.

And soon a little chaos develops.

Where is that great recipe I wanted to make as soon as tomatoes were in season? What did I do with that recipe I made for the neighbors, and they asked to take the leftovers home? Which book has the chocolate dessert recipe that our daughter asked me to fix for her birthday?

"Where Is That Recipe?" is your personal index to your favorite recipes.

Spend your time cooking instead of searching!

Appetizers and Snacks

Name of Recipe	Recipe Source	Page Number in Book or Magazine

Appetizers and Snacks

Name of Recipe	Recipe Source	Page Number in Book or Magazine
....	....	....
....	....	....
....	....	....
....	....	....
....	....	....
....	....	....
....	....	....
....	....	....
....	....	....
....	....	....
....	....	....
....	....	....
....	....	....
....	....	....
....	....	....
....	....	....
....	....	....
....	....	....
....	....	....
....	....	....
....	....	....

Appetizers and Snacks

Name of Recipe	Recipe Source	Page Number in Book or Magazine

Appetizers and Snacks

Name of Recipe	Recipe Source	Page Number in Book or Magazine
....	....	....
....	....	....
....	....	....
....	....	....
....	....	....
....	....	....
....	....	....
....	....	....
....	....	....
....	....	....
....	....	....
....	....	....
....	....	....
....	....	....
....	....	....
....	....	....
....	....	....
....	....	....
....	....	....
....	....	....
....	....	....
....	....	....
....	....	....

Breads and Muffins

Name of Recipe	Recipe Source	Page Number in Book or Magazine

Breads and Muffins

Name of Recipe	Recipe Source	Page Number in Book or Magazine

Breads and Muffins

Name of Recipe	Recipe Source	Page Number in Book or Magazine

Jellies, Jams, and Preserves

Name of Recipe	Recipe Source	Page Number in Book or Magazine

Breakfasts and Brunches

Name of Recipe	Recipe Source	Page Number in Book or Magazine

Breakfasts and Brunches

Name of Recipe	Recipe Source	Page Number in Book or Magazine

Soups, Stews, and Chilis

Name of Recipe	Recipe Source	Page Number in Book or Magazine

Soups, Stews, and Chilis

Name of Recipe	Recipe Source	Page Number in Book or Magazine

Soups, Stews, and Chilis

Name of Recipe	Recipe Source	Page Number in Book or Magazine

Soups, Stews, and Chilis

Name of Recipe	Recipe Source	Page Number in Book or Magazine

Salads and Salad Dressings

Name of Recipe	Recipe Source	Page Number in Book or Magazine

Salads and Salad Dressings

Name of Recipe	Recipe Source	Page Number in Book or Magazine
....	....	....
....	....	....
....	....	....
....	....	....
....	....	....
....	....	....
....	....	....
....	....	....
....	....	....
....	....	....
....	....	....
....	....	....
....	....	....
....	....	....
....	....	....
....	....	....
....	....	....
....	....	....
....	....	....
....	....	....
....	....	....
....	....	....
....	....	....
....	....	....

Salads and Salad Dressings

Name of Recipe	Recipe Source	Page Number in Book or Magazine

Salads and Salad Dressings

Name of Recipe	Recipe Source	Page Number in Book or Magazine

Salads and Salad Dressings

Name of Recipe	Recipe Source	Page Number in Book or Magazine

Vegetables

Name of Recipe	Recipe Source	Page Number in Book or Magazine
....	....	....
....	....	....
....	....	....
....	....	....
....	....	....
....	....	....
....	....	....
....	....	....
....	....	....
....	....	....
....	....	....
....	....	....
....	....	....
....	....	....
....	....	....
....	....	....
....	....	....
....	....	....
....	....	....
....	....	....
....	....	....
....	....	....

Vegetables

Name of Recipe	Recipe Source	Page Number in Book or Magazine

Vegetables

Name of Recipe	Recipe Source	Page Number in Book or Magazine

Vegetables

Name of Recipe	Recipe Source	Page Number in Book or Magazine
....	....	....
....	....	....
....	....	....
....	....	....
....	....	....
....	....	....
....	....	....
....	....	....
....	....	....
....	....	....
....	....	....
....	....	....
....	....	....
....	....	....
....	....	....
....	....	....
....	....	....
....	....	....
....	....	....
....	....	....
....	....	....
....	....	....
....	....	....

Vegetables

Name of Recipe	Recipe Source	Page Number in Book or Magazine

Meats: Chicken and Turkey

Name of Recipe	Recipe Source	Page Number in Book or Magazine

Meats: Chicken and Turkey

Name of Recipe	Recipe Source	Page Number in Book or Magazine
....	....	....
....	....	....
....	....	....
....	....	....
....	....	....
....	....	....
....	....	....
....	....	....
....	....	....
....	....	....
....	....	....
....	....	....
....	....	....
....	....	....
....	....	....
....	....	....
....	....	....
....	....	....
....	....	....
....	....	....
....	....	....

Meats: Chicken and Turkey

Name of Recipe	Recipe Source	Page Number in Book or Magazine

Meats: Pork

Name of Recipe	Recipe Source	Page Number in Book or Magazine
....	....	....
....	....	....
....	....	....
....	....	....
....	....	....
....	....	....
....	....	....
....	....	....
....	....	....
....	....	....
....	....	....
....	....	....
....	....	....
....	....	....
....	....	....
....	....	....
....	....	....
....	....	....
....	....	....
....	....	....
....	....	....
....	....	....
....	....	....

Meats: Pork

Name of Recipe	Recipe Source	Page Number in Book or Magazine

Meats: Beef

Name of Recipe	Recipe Source	Page Number in Book or Magazine
....	....	....
....	....	....
....	....	....
....	....	....
....	....	....
....	....	....
....	....	....
....	....	....
....	....	....
....	....	....
....	....	....
....	....	....
....	....	....
....	....	....
....	....	....
....	....	....
....	....	....
....	....	....
....	....	....
....	....	....
....	....	....
....	....	....
....	....	....
....	....	....
....	....	....

Meats: Beef

Name of Recipe	Recipe Source	Page Number in Book or Magazine

Meats: Beef

Name of Recipe	Recipe Source	Page Number in Book or Magazine
....	....	....
....	....	....
....	....	....
....	....	....
....	....	....
....	....	....
....	....	....
....	....	....
....	....	....
....	....	....
....	....	....
....	....	....
....	....	....
....	....	....
....	....	....
....	....	....
....	....	....
....	....	....
....	....	....
....	....	....
....	....	....

Meats: Lamb

Name of Recipe	Recipe Source	Page Number in Book or Magazine

Meats: Others

Name of Recipe	Recipe Source	Page Number in Book or Magazine
....	....	....
....	....	....
....	....	....
....	....	....
....	....	....
....	....	....
....	....	....
....	....	....
....	....	....
....	....	....
....	....	....
....	....	....
....	....	....
....	....	....
....	....	....
....	....	....
....	....	....
....	....	....
....	....	....
....	....	....
....	....	....
....	....	....

Meats: Others

Name of Recipe	Recipe Source	Page Number in Book or Magazine

Seafood

Name of Recipe	Recipe Source	Page Number in Book or Magazine
....	....	....
....	....	....
....	....	....
....	....	....
....	....	....
....	....	....
....	....	....
....	....	....
....	....	....
....	....	....
....	....	....
....	....	....
....	....	....
....	....	....
....	....	....
....	....	....
....	....	....
....	....	....
....	....	....
....	....	....
....	....	....
....	....	....
....	....	....

Seafood

Name of Recipe	Recipe Source	Page Number in Book or Magazine

Meatless Main Dishes

Name of Recipe	Recipe Source	Page Number in Book or Magazine

Meatless Main Dishes

Name of Recipe	Recipe Source	Page Number in Book or Magazine

Meatless Main Dishes

Name of Recipe	Recipe Source	Page Number in Book or Magazine

Pastas and Pizzas

Name of Recipe	Recipe Source	Page Number in Book or Magazine

Pastas and Pizzas

Name of Recipe	Recipe Source	Page Number in Book or Magazine

Pastas and Pizzas

Name of Recipe	Recipe Source	Page Number in Book or Magazine

Grilling

Name of Recipe	Recipe Source	Page Number in Book or Magazine

Sandwiches

Name of Recipe	Recipe Source	Page Number in Book or Magazine

Casseroles

Name of Recipe	Recipe Source	Page Number in Book or Magazine

Casseroles

Name of Recipe	Recipe Source	Page Number in Book or Magazine

Casseroles

Name of Recipe	Recipe Source	Page Number in Book or Magazine

Cakes and Frostings

Name of Recipe	Recipe Source	Page Number in Book or Magazine

Cakes and Frostings

Name of Recipe	Recipe Source	Page Number in Book or Magazine

Cakes and Frostings

Name of Recipe	Recipe Source	Page Number in Book or Magazine

Pies

Name of Recipe	Recipe Source	Page Number in Book or Magazine

Pies

Name of Recipe	Recipe Source	Page Number in Book or Magazine
....	....	....
....	....	....
....	....	....
....	....	....
....	....	....
....	....	....
....	....	....
....	....	....
....	....	....
....	....	....
....	....	....
....	....	....
....	....	....
....	....	....
....	....	....
....	....	....
....	....	....
....	....	....
....	....	....
....	....	....
....	....	....
....	....	....
....	....	....

Pies

Name of Recipe	Recipe Source	Page Number in Book or Magazine

Cookies and Bars

Name of Recipe	Recipe Source	Page Number in Book or Magazine

Cookies and Bars

Name of Recipe	Recipe Source	Page Number in Book or Magazine

Cookies and Bars

Name of Recipe	Recipe Source	Page Number in Book or Magazine

Crisps, Cobblers, and Puddings

Name of Recipe	Recipe Source	Page Number in Book or Magazine

Crisps, Cobblers, and Puddings

Name of Recipe	Recipe Source	Page Number in Book or Magazine

Other Desserts

Name of Recipe	Recipe Source	Page Number in Book or Magazine
....	....	....
....	....	....
....	....	....
....	....	....
....	....	....
....	....	....
....	....	....
....	....	....
....	....	....
....	....	....
....	....	....
....	....	....
....	....	....
....	....	....
....	....	....
....	....	....
....	....	....
....	....	....
....	....	....
....	....	....
....	....	....
....	....	....
....	....	....

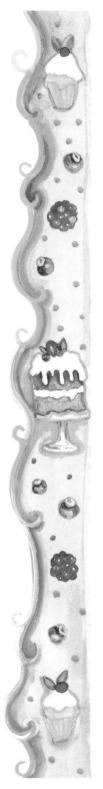

Other Desserts

Name of Recipe	Recipe Source	Page Number in Book or Magazine

Beverages

Name of Recipe	Recipe Source	Page Number in Book or Magazine

Beverages

Name of Recipe	Recipe Source	Page Number in Book or Magazine

Candies

Name of Recipe	Recipe Source	Page Number in Book or Magazine
....	....	....
....	....	....
....	....	....
....	....	....
....	....	....
....	....	....
....	....	....
....	....	....
....	....	....
....	....	....
....	....	....
....	....	....
....	....	....
....	....	....
....	....	....
....	....	....
....	....	....
....	....	....
....	....	....
....	....	....
....	....	....
....	....	....

Food I've Served to Family and Friends

For years I've scribbled notes on scrap paper each time we've had guests for a meal, writing who had come and what I made for them. I often go back through my mismatched papers, bunched together with rubber bands, to remind myself of great menus I've forgotten about.

Now I will have all those notes in one place—in this "entertainment diary"—saving me from another time-wasting hunt.

And there's space, too, to record where those recipes can be found.

So, no more need to worry about duplicating the meal you made the last time your friends came for dinner.

And no more scrounging through your memory about what you've prepared for your family's traditional holiday spreads. You have it all recorded in your personal *Cook's Journal!*

Food I've Served to Family and Friends

Date ....   Time of Day ....

The Occasion ....

Guest List

....

....

....

....

Menu	Recipe Source (and page number)	Comments (about this dish on this occasion)
....	....	....
....	....	....
....	....	....
....	....	....
....	....	....

Decorations (Centerpiece, colors, linens used, flowers, candles, other speical touches)

....

....

....

This menu works well because:
- ❏ It always brings good comments
- ❏ Everything is fresh and seasonal
- ❏ Other reasons ....

- ❏ Quick to prepare
- ❏ Kids like it
- ❏ It's unusual

- ❏ Flavors are well balanced
- ❏ Free of last-minute stress
- ❏ Great party or celebration meal

This menu is especially good for:
- ❏ Thanksgiving
- ❏ Old friends
- ❏ Other reasons ....

- ❏ Christmas
- ❏ New friends

- ❏ Birthdays
- ❏ Easter
- ❏ Neighbors

- ❏ Sunday lunches
- ❏ Picnics
- ❏ Colleagues

- ❏ After the game
- ❏ Cooking Club

Food I've Served to Family and Friends

Date .... Time of Day ....

The Occasion ....

Guest List

....
....
....
....

Menu	Recipe Source (and page number)	Comments (about this dish)
....	....	....
....	....	....
....	....	....
....	....	....
....	....	....

Decorations (Centerpiece, colors, linens used, flowers, candles, other speical touches)

....
....
....

This menu works well because:
- ❏ Quick to prepare
- ❏ Flavors are well balanced
- ❏ It always brings good comments
- ❏ Kids like it
- ❏ Free of last-minute stress
- ❏ Everything is fresh and seasonal
- ❏ It's unusual
- ❏ Great party or celebration meal
- ❏ Other reasons ....

This menu is especially good for:
- ❏ Birthdays
- ❏ Sunday lunches
- ❏ After the game
- ❏ Thanksgiving
- ❏ Christmas
- ❏ Easter
- ❏ Picnics
- ❏ Cooking Club
- ❏ Old friends
- ❏ New friends
- ❏ Neighbors
- ❏ Colleagues
- ❏ Other reasons ....

Food I've Served to Family and Friends

Date .... Time of Day ....
The Occasion ....

Guest List

....
....
....
                                          ....

Menu   Recipe Source   Comments
                     (and page number)   (about this dish)

....
....
....
....
....

Decorations (Centerpiece, colors, linens used, other speical touches)

....
....
....

This menu works well because: ❑ Quick to prepare   ❑ Flavors are well balanced
❑ It always brings good comments ❑ Kids like it   ❑ Free of last-minute stress
❑ Everything is fresh and seasonal ❑ It's unusual   ❑ Great party or celebration meal
❑ Other reasons ....

This menu is especially good for: ❑ Birthdays   ❑ Sunday lunches   ❑ After the game
❑ Thanksgiving   ❑ Christmas   ❑ Easter   ❑ Picnics   ❑ Cooking Club
❑ Old friends   ❑ New friends   ❑ Neighbors   ❑ Colleagues
❑ Other reasons ....

Food I've Served to Family and Friends

Date .... Time of Day ....

The Occasion ....

Guest List

....

....

....

....

Menu	Recipe Source (and page number)	Comments (about this dish on this occasion)
....	....	....
....	....	....
....	....	....
....	....	....
....	....	....

Decorations (Centerpiece, colors, linens used, flowers, candles, other speical touches)

....

....

....

This menu works well because: ❑ Quick to prepare ❑ Flavors are well balanced

❑ It always brings good comments ❑ Kids like it ❑ Free of last-minute stress

❑ Everything is fresh and seasonal ❑ It's unusual ❑ Great party or celebration meal

❑ Other reasons ....

This menu is especially good for: ❑ Birthdays ❑ Sunday lunches ❑ After the game

❑ Thanksgiving ❑ Christmas ❑ Easter ❑ Picnics ❑ Cooking Club

❑ Old friends ❑ New friends ❑ Neighbors ❑ Colleagues

❑ Other reasons ....

Food I've Served to Family and Friends

Date .... Time of Day ....
The Occasion ....

Guest List

....
....
....
....

Menu	Recipe Source (and page number)	Comments (about this dish on this occasion)
....	....	....
....	....	....
....	....	....

Decorations (Centerpiece, colors, flowers, linens used, candles, other speical touches)
....
....
....
....

This menu works well because:
❑ Quick to prepare ❑ Flavors are well balanced
❑ It always brings good comments ❑ Kids like it ❑ Free of last-minute stress
❑ Everything is fresh and seasonal ❑ It's unusual ❑ Great party or celebration meal
❑ Other reasons ....

This menu is especially good for:
❑ Birthdays ❑ Sunday lunches ❑ After the game
❑ Thanksgiving ❑ Christmas ❑ Easter ❑ Picnics ❑ Cooking Club
❑ Old friends ❑ New friends ❑ Neighbors ❑ Colleagues
❑ Other reasons ....

Food I've Served to Family and Friends

Date .... Time of Day ....

The Occasion ....

Guest List

....

....

....

....

Menu	Recipe Source (and page number)	Comments (about this dish)
....	....	....
....	....	....
....	....	....
....	....	....
....	....	....

Decorations (Centerpiece, colors, linens used, flowers, candles, other speical touches)

....

....

....

This menu works well because:
- ❑ Quick to prepare
- ❑ Flavors are well balanced
- ❑ It always brings good comments
- ❑ Kids like it
- ❑ Free of last-minute stress
- ❑ Everything is fresh and seasonal
- ❑ It's unusual
- ❑ Great party or celebration meal
- ❑ Other reasons ....

This menu is especially good for:
- ❑ Birthdays
- ❑ Sunday lunches
- ❑ After the game
- ❑ Thanksgiving
- ❑ Christmas
- ❑ Easter
- ❑ Picnics
- ❑ Cooking Club
- ❑ Old friends
- ❑ New friends
- ❑ Neighbors
- ❑ Colleagues
- ❑ Other reasons ....

Food I've Served to Family and Friends

Date .... Time of Day ....

The Occasion ....

Guest List

....

....

....

....

Menu	Recipe Source (and page number)	Comments (about this dish)
....	....	....
....	....	....
....	....	....
....	....	....
....	....	....

Decorations (Centerpiece, colors, linens used, flowers, candles, other speical touches)

....

....

....

This menu works well because: ❑ Quick to prepare ❑ Flavors are well balanced

❑ It always brings good comments ❑ Kids like it ❑ Free of last-minute stress

❑ Everything is fresh and seasonal ❑ It's unusual ❑ Great party or celebration meal

❑ Other reasons ....

This menu is especially good for: ❑ Birthdays ❑ Sunday lunches ❑ After the game

❑ Thanksgiving ❑ Christmas ❑ Easter ❑ Picnics ❑ Cooking Club

❑ Old friends ❑ New friends ❑ Neighbors ❑ Colleagues

❑ Other reasons ....

Food I've Served to Family and Friends

Date .... Time of Day ....

The Occasion ....

Guest List

....

....

....

....

Menu	Recipe Source (and page number)	Comments (about this dish on this occasion)
....	....	....
....	....	....
....	....	....

Decorations (Centerpiece, colors, flowers, linens used, candles, other speical touches)

....

....

....

....

This menu works well because:

❑ It always brings good comments

❑ Everything is fresh and seasonal

❑ Other reasons ....

❑ Quick to prepare

❑ Kids like it

❑ It's unusual

❑ Flavors are well balanced

❑ Free of last-minute stress

❑ Great party or celebration meal

This menu is especially good for:

❑ Birthdays   ❑ Sunday lunches   ❑ After the game

❑ Thanksgiving   ❑ Christmas   ❑ Easter   ❑ Picnics   ❑ Cooking Club

❑ Old friends   ❑ New friends   ❑ Neighbors   ❑ Colleagues

❑ Other reasons ....

Food I've Served to Family and Friends

Date .... Time of Day ....

The Occasion ....

Guest List

....

....

....

....

Menu	Recipe Source (and page number)	Comments (about this dish on this occasion)
....	....	....
....	....	....
....	....	....
....	....	....
....	....	....

Decorations (Centerpiece, colors, linens used, flowers, candles, other speical touches)

....

....

....

This menu works well because:
❑ Quick to prepare   ❑ Flavors are well balanced
❑ It always brings good comments   ❑ Kids like it   ❑ Free of last-minute stress
❑ Everything is fresh and seasonal   ❑ It's unusual   ❑ Great party or celebration meal
❑ Other reasons ....

This menu is especially good for:
❑ Birthdays   ❑ Sunday lunches   ❑ After the game
❑ Thanksgiving   ❑ Christmas   ❑ Easter   ❑ Picnics   ❑ Cooking Club
❑ Old friends   ❑ New friends   ❑ Neighbors   ❑ Colleagues
❑ Other reasons ....

Food I've Served to Family and Friends

Date .... Time of Day ....

The Occasion ....

Guest List

....

....

....

....

Menu	Recipe Source (and page number)	Comments (about this dish on this occasion)
....	....	....
....	....	....
....	....	....

Decorations (Centerpiece, colors, flowers, linens used, candles, other speical touches)

....

....

....

....

This menu works well because:
- ❏ Quick to prepare
- ❏ Flavors are well balanced
- ❏ It always brings good comments
- ❏ Kids like it
- ❏ Free of last-minute stress
- ❏ Everything is fresh and seasonal
- ❏ It's unusual
- ❏ Great party or celebration meal
- ❏ Other reasons ....

This menu is especially good for:
- ❏ Birthdays
- ❏ Sunday lunches
- ❏ After the game
- ❏ Thanksgiving
- ❏ Christmas
- ❏ Easter
- ❏ Picnics
- ❏ Cooking Club
- ❏ Old friends
- ❏ New friends
- ❏ Neighbors
- ❏ Colleagues
- ❏ Other reasons ....

Food I've Served to Family and Friends

Date .... Time of Day ....

The Occasion ....

Guest List

....

....

....

....

Menu   Recipe Source   Comments
                      (and page number)   (about this dish)

....

....

....

....

....

Decorations (Centerpiece, colors, linens used, other speical touches)

....

....

....

This menu works well because: ❑ Quick to prepare   ❑ Flavors are well balanced

❑ It always brings good comments   ❑ Kids like it   ❑ Free of last-minute stress

❑ Everything is fresh and seasonal   ❑ It's unusual   ❑ Great party or celebration meal

❑ Other reasons ....

This menu is especially good for: ❑ Birthdays   ❑ Sunday lunches   ❑ After the game

❑ Thanksgiving   ❑ Christmas   ❑ Easter   ❑ Picnics   ❑ Cooking Club

❑ Old friends   ❑ New friends   ❑ Neighbors   ❑ Colleagues

❑ Other reasons ....

Food I've Served to Family and Friends

Date .... Time of Day ....
The Occasion ....

Guest List

....
....
....
....

Menu	Recipe Source (and page number)	Comments (about this dish)
....	....	....
....	....	....
....	....	....
....	....	....
....	....	....

Decorations (Centerpiece, colors, linens used, flowers, candles, other speical touches)

....
....
....

This menu works well because:
- ❏ Quick to prepare
- ❏ Flavors are well balanced
- ❏ It always brings good comments
- ❏ Kids like it
- ❏ Free of last-minute stress
- ❏ Everything is fresh and seasonal
- ❏ It's unusual
- ❏ Great party or celebration meal
- ❏ Other reasons ....

This menu is especially good for:
- ❏ Birthdays
- ❏ Sunday lunches
- ❏ After the game
- ❏ Thanksgiving
- ❏ Christmas
- ❏ Easter
- ❏ Picnics
- ❏ Cooking Club
- ❏ Old friends
- ❏ New friends
- ❏ Neighbors
- ❏ Colleagues
- ❏ Other reasons ....

Food I've Served to Family and Friends

Date .... Time of Day ....

The Occasion ....

Guest List

....

....

....

....

Menu	Recipe Source (and page number)	Comments (about this dish on this occasion)
....	....	....
....	....	....
....	....	....

Decorations (Centerpiece, colors, flowers, linens used, candles, other speical touches)

....

....

....

....

This menu works well because:

❑ It always brings good comments   ❑ Quick to prepare   ❑ Flavors are well balanced

❑ Everything is fresh and seasonal   ❑ Kids like it   ❑ Free of last-minute stress

❑ Other reasons ....   ❑ It's unusual   ❑ Great party or celebration meal

This menu is especially good for:

❑ Birthdays   ❑ Sunday lunches   ❑ After the game

❑ Thanksgiving   ❑ Christmas   ❑ Easter   ❑ Picnics   ❑ Cooking Club

❑ Old friends   ❑ New friends   ❑ Neighbors   ❑ Colleagues

❑ Other reasons ....

Food I've Served to Family and Friends

Date .... Time of Day ....

The Occasion ....

Guest List

....

....

....

....

Menu	Recipe Source (and page number)	Comments (about this dish)
....	....	....
....	....	....
....	....	....
....	....	....
....		

Decorations (Centerpiece, colors, linens used, flowers, candles, other speical touches)

....

....

....

This menu works well because: ❑ Quick to prepare   ❑ Flavors are well balanced

❑ It always brings good comments   ❑ Kids like it   ❑ Free of last-minute stress

❑ Everything is fresh and seasonal   ❑ It's unusual   ❑ Great party or celebration meal

❑ Other reasons ....

This menu is especially good for: ❑ Birthdays   ❑ Sunday lunches   ❑ After the game

❑ Thanksgiving   ❑ Christmas   ❑ Easter   ❑ Picnics   ❑ Cooking Club

❑ Old friends   ❑ New friends   ❑ Neighbors   ❑ Colleagues

❑ Other reasons ....

Food I've Served to Family and Friends

Date .... Time of Day ....

The Occasion ....

Guest List

....

....

....

....

Menu	Recipe Source (and page number)	Comments (about this dish on this occasion)
....	....	....
....	....	....
....	....	....

Decorations (Centerpiece, colors, flowers, linens used, candles, other speical touches)

....

....

....

....

This menu works well because: ❑ Quick to prepare   ❑ Flavors are well balanced

❑ It always brings good comments   ❑ Kids like it   ❑ Free of last-minute stress

❑ Everything is fresh and seasonal   ❑ It's unusual   ❑ Great party or celebration meal

❑ Other reasons ....

This menu is especially good for: ❑ Birthdays   ❑ Sunday lunches   ❑ After the game

❑ Thanksgiving   ❑ Christmas   ❑ Easter   ❑ Picnics   ❑ Cooking Club

❑ Old friends   ❑ New friends   ❑ Neighbors   ❑ Colleagues

❑ Other reasons ....

Food I've Served to Family and Friends

Date .... Time of Day ....

The Occasion ....

Guest List

....

....

....

....

Menu	Recipe Source (and page number)	Comments (about this dish)
....	....	....
....	....	....
....	....	....
....	....	....
....	....	....

Decorations (Centerpiece, colors, linens used, flowers, candles, other speical touches)

....

....

....

This menu works well because:
- ❏ Quick to prepare
- ❏ Flavors are well balanced
- ❏ It always brings good comments
- ❏ Kids like it
- ❏ Free of last-minute stress
- ❏ Everything is fresh and seasonal
- ❏ It's unusual
- ❏ Great party or celebration meal
- ❏ Other reasons ....

This menu is especially good for:
- ❏ Birthdays
- ❏ Sunday lunches
- ❏ After the game
- ❏ Thanksgiving
- ❏ Christmas
- ❏ Easter
- ❏ Picnics
- ❏ Cooking Club
- ❏ Old friends
- ❏ New friends
- ❏ Neighbors
- ❏ Colleagues
- ❏ Other reasons ....

Food I've Served to Family and Friends

Date .... Time of Day ....

The Occasion ....

Guest List

....

....

....

                                                  ....

Menu	Recipe Source (and page number)	Comments (about this dish)
....	....	....
....	....	....
....	....	....
....	....	....

Decorations (Centerpiece, colors, linens used, other speical touches)

....

....

....

This menu works well because: ❑ Quick to prepare   ❑ Flavors are well balanced

❑ It always brings good comments ❑ Kids like it   ❑ Free of last-minute stress

❑ Everything is fresh and seasonal ❑ It's unusual   ❑ Great party or celebration meal

❑ Other reasons ....

This menu is especially good for: ❑ Birthdays   ❑ Sunday lunches   ❑ After the game

❑ Thanksgiving   ❑ Christmas   ❑ Easter   ❑ Picnics   ❑ Cooking Club

❑ Old friends   ❑ New friends   ❑ Neighbors   ❑ Colleagues

❑ Other reasons ....

Food I've Served to Family and Friends

Date .... Time of Day ....

The Occasion ....

Guest List

....

....

....

....

Menu   Recipe Source   Comments
                            (and page number)   (about this dish on this occasion)

....

....

....

....

....

Decorations (Centerpiece, colors, linens used, flowers, candles, other speical touches)

....

....

....

This menu works well because: ❑ Quick to prepare   ❑ Flavors are well balanced

❑ It always brings good comments   ❑ Kids like it   ❑ Free of last-minute stress

❑ Everything is fresh and seasonal ❑ It's unusual   ❑ Great party or celebration meal

❑ Other reasons ....

This menu is especially good for: ❑ Birthdays   ❑ Sunday lunches   ❑ After the game

❑ Thanksgiving   ❑ Christmas   ❑ Easter   ❑ Picnics   ❑ Cooking Club

❑ Old friends   ❑ New friends   ❑ Neighbors   ❑ Colleagues

❑ Other reasons ....

Food I've Served to Family and Friends

Date .... Time of Day ....

The Occasion ....

Guest List

....

....

....

....

Menu   Recipe Source   Comments
                            (and page number)   (about this dish on this occasion)

....

....

....

Decorations (Centerpiece, colors, flowers,
linens used, candles, other speical touches)

....

....

....

....

This menu works well because: ❑ Quick to prepare   ❑ Flavors are well balanced

❑ It always brings good comments   ❑ Kids like it   ❑ Free of last-minute stress

❑ Everything is fresh and seasonal ❑ It's unusual   ❑ Great party or celebration meal

❑ Other reasons ....

This menu is especially good for: ❑ Birthdays   ❑ Sunday lunches   ❑ After the game

❑ Thanksgiving   ❑ Christmas   ❑ Easter   ❑ Picnics   ❑ Cooking Club

❑ Old friends   ❑ New friends   ❑ Neighbors   ❑ Colleagues

❑ Other reasons ....

Food I've Served to Family and Friends

Date .... Time of Day ....

The Occasion ....

Guest List

....

....

....

....

Menu	Recipe Source (and page number)	Comments (about this dish)
....	....	....
....	....	....
....	....	....
....	....	....
....	....	....

Decorations (Centerpiece, colors, linens used, flowers, candles, other speical touches)

....

....

....

This menu works well because: ❏ Quick to prepare ❏ Flavors are well balanced

❏ It always brings good comments ❏ Kids like it ❏ Free of last-minute stress

❏ Everything is fresh and seasonal ❏ It's unusual ❏ Great party or celebration meal

❏ Other reasons ....

This menu is especially good for: ❏ Birthdays ❏ Sunday lunches ❏ After the game

❏ Thanksgiving ❏ Christmas ❏ Easter ❏ Picnics ❏ Cooking Club

❏ Old friends ❏ New friends ❏ Neighbors ❏ Colleagues

❏ Other reasons ....

Food I've Served to Family and Friends

Date .... Time of Day ....
The Occasion ....

Guest List

....
....
....
....

Menu   Recipe Source   Comments
                      (and page number)   (about this dish)

....
....
....
....

Decorations (Centerpiece, colors, linens used, flowers, candles, other speical touches)

....
....
....

This menu works well because: ❑ Quick to prepare   ❑ Flavors are well balanced

❑ It always brings good comments ❑ Kids like it   ❑ Free of last-minute stress

❑ Everything is fresh and seasonal ❑ It's unusual   ❑ Great party or celebration meal

❑ Other reasons ....

This menu is especially good for: ❑ Birthdays   ❑ Sunday lunches   ❑ After the game

❑ Thanksgiving   ❑ Christmas   ❑ Easter   ❑ Picnics   ❑ Cooking Club

❑ Old friends   ❑ New friends   ❑ Neighbors   ❑ Colleagues

❑ Other reasons ....

Food I've Served to Family and Friends

Date .... Time of Day ....

The Occasion ....

Guest List

....
....
....
....

Menu	Recipe Source (and page number)	Comments (about this dish on this occasion)
....	....	....
....	....	....
....	....	....
....	....	....
....	....	....

Decorations (Centerpiece, colors, linens used, flowers, candles, other speical touches)

....
....
....

This menu works well because: ❏ Quick to prepare ❏ Flavors are well balanced

❏ It always brings good comments ❏ Kids like it ❏ Free of last-minute stress

❏ Everything is fresh and seasonal ❏ It's unusual ❏ Great party or celebration meal

❏ Other reasons ....

This menu is especially good for: ❏ Birthdays ❏ Sunday lunches ❏ After the game

❏ Thanksgiving ❏ Christmas ❏ Easter ❏ Picnics ❏ Cooking Club

❏ Old friends ❏ New friends ❏ Neighbors ❏ Colleagues

❏ Other reasons ....

Food I've Served to Family and Friends

Date ....   Time of Day ....

The Occasion ....

Guest List

....

....

....

....

Menu	Recipe Source (and page number)	Comments (about this dish on this occasion)
....	....	....
....	....	....
....	....	....

Decorations (Centerpiece, colors, flowers, linens used, candles, other speical touches)

....

....

....

....

This menu works well because:

❑ It always brings good comments

❑ Everything is fresh and seasonal

❑ Other reasons ....

❑ Quick to prepare

❑ Kids like it

❑ It's unusual

❑ Flavors are well balanced

❑ Free of last-minute stress

❑ Great party or celebration meal

This menu is especially good for:

❑ Birthdays   ❑ Sunday lunches   ❑ After the game

❑ Thanksgiving   ❑ Christmas   ❑ Easter   ❑ Picnics   ❑ Cooking Club

❑ Old friends   ❑ New friends   ❑ Neighbors   ❑ Colleagues

❑ Other reasons ....

94

Food I've Served to Family and Friends

Date .... Time of Day ....

The Occasion ....

Guest List

....

....

....

....

Menu	Recipe Source (and page number)	Comments (about this dish)
....	....	....
....	....	....
....	....	....
....	....	....
....	....	....

Decorations (Centerpiece, colors, linens used, flowers, candles, other speical touches)

....

....

....

This menu works well because:
- ❑ It always brings good comments
- ❑ Everything is fresh and seasonal
- ❑ Quick to prepare
- ❑ Kids like it
- ❑ It's unusual
- ❑ Flavors are well balanced
- ❑ Free of last-minute stress
- ❑ Great party or celebration meal
- ❑ Other reasons ....

This menu is especially good for:
- ❑ Birthdays
- ❑ Sunday lunches
- ❑ After the game
- ❑ Thanksgiving
- ❑ Christmas
- ❑ Easter
- ❑ Picnics
- ❑ Cooking Club
- ❑ Old friends
- ❑ New friends
- ❑ Neighbors
- ❑ Colleagues
- ❑ Other reasons ....

Food I've Served to Family and Friends

Date .... Time of Day ....

The Occasion ....

Guest List

....

....

....

....

Menu	Recipe Source (and page number)	Comments (about this dish on this occasion)
....	....	....
....	....	....
....	....	....

Decorations (Centerpiece, colors, flowers, linens used, candles, other speical touches)

....

....

....

....

This menu works well because:
- ❑ Quick to prepare
- ❑ Flavors are well balanced
- ❑ It always brings good comments
- ❑ Kids like it
- ❑ Free of last-minute stress
- ❑ Everything is fresh and seasonal
- ❑ It's unusual
- ❑ Great party or celebration meal
- ❑ Other reasons ....

This menu is especially good for:
- ❑ Birthdays
- ❑ Sunday lunches
- ❑ After the game
- ❑ Thanksgiving
- ❑ Christmas
- ❑ Easter
- ❑ Picnics
- ❑ Cooking Club
- ❑ Old friends
- ❑ New friends
- ❑ Neighbors
- ❑ Colleagues
- ❑ Other reasons ....

96

Food I've Served to Family and Friends

Date ....   Time of Day ....

The Occasion ....

Guest List

....

....

....

....

Menu	Recipe Source (and page number)	Comments (about this dish on this occasion)
....	....	....
....	....	....
....	....	....
....	....	....
....	....	....

Decorations (Centerpiece, colors, linens used, flowers, candles, other speical touches)

....

....

....

This menu works well because:
- ❑ Quick to prepare
- ❑ Flavors are well balanced
- ❑ It always brings good comments
- ❑ Kids like it
- ❑ Free of last-minute stress
- ❑ Everything is fresh and seasonal
- ❑ It's unusual
- ❑ Great party or celebration meal
- ❑ Other reasons ....

This menu is especially good for:
- ❑ Birthdays
- ❑ Sunday lunches
- ❑ After the game
- ❑ Thanksgiving
- ❑ Christmas
- ❑ Easter
- ❑ Picnics
- ❑ Cooking Club
- ❑ Old friends
- ❑ New friends
- ❑ Neighbors
- ❑ Colleagues
- ❑ Other reasons ....

Food I've Served to Family and Friends

Date .... Time of Day ....
The Occasion ....

Guest List

....
....
....
....

Menu	Recipe Source (and page number)	Comments (about this dish)
....	....	....
....	....	....
....	....	....
....	....	....
....	....	....

Decorations (Centerpiece, colors, linens used, flowers, candles, other speical touches)

....
....
....

This menu works well because: ❑ Quick to prepare   ❑ Flavors are well balanced
❑ It always brings good comments   ❑ Kids like it   ❑ Free of last-minute stress
❑ Everything is fresh and seasonal   ❑ It's unusual   ❑ Great party or celebration meal
❑ Other reasons ....

This menu is especially good for: ❑ Birthdays   ❑ Sunday lunches   ❑ After the game
❑ Thanksgiving   ❑ Christmas   ❑ Easter   ❑ Picnics   ❑ Cooking Club
❑ Old friends   ❑ New friends   ❑ Neighbors   ❑ Colleagues
❑ Other reasons ....

Food I've Served to Family and Friends

Date .... Time of Day ....

The Occasion ....

Guest List

....
....
....
....

Menu   Recipe Source   Comments
                            (and page number)   (about this dish on this occasion)

....
....
....

Decorations (Centerpiece, colors, flowers,
linens used, candles, other speical touches)

....

....

....

....

This menu works well because: ❏ Quick to prepare   ❏ Flavors are well balanced

❏ It always brings good comments   ❏ Kids like it   ❏ Free of last-minute stress

❏ Everything is fresh and seasonal ❏ It's unusual   ❏ Great party or celebration meal

❏ Other reasons ....

This menu is especially good for: ❏ Birthdays   ❏ Sunday lunches   ❏ After the game

❏ Thanksgiving   ❏ Christmas   ❏ Easter   ❏ Picnics   ❏ Cooking Club

❏ Old friends   ❏ New friends   ❏ Neighbors   ❏ Colleagues

❏ Other reasons ....

Food I've Served to Family and Friends

Date .... Time of Day ....

The Occasion ....

Guest List

....

....

....

....

Menu	Recipe Source (and page number)	Comments (about this dish)
....	....	....
....	....	....
....	....	....
....	....	....
....	....	....

Decorations (Centerpiece, colors, linens used, flowers, candles, other speical touches)

....

....

....

This menu works well because: ❑ Quick to prepare   ❑ Flavors are well balanced

❑ It always brings good comments   ❑ Kids like it   ❑ Free of last-minute stress

❑ Everything is fresh and seasonal ❑ It's unusual   ❑ Great party or celebration meal

❑ Other reasons ....

This menu is especially good for: ❑ Birthdays   ❑ Sunday lunches   ❑ After the game

❑ Thanksgiving   ❑ Christmas   ❑ Easter   ❑ Picnics   ❑ Cooking Club

❑ Old friends   ❑ New friends   ❑ Neighbors   ❑ Colleagues

❑ Other reasons ....

Food I've Served to Family and Friends

Date .... Time of Day ....

The Occasion ....

Guest List

....

....

....

....

Menu	Recipe Source (and page number)	Comments (about this dish)
....	....	....
....	....	....
....	....	....
....	....	....
....	....	....

Decorations (Centerpiece, colors, linens used, other speical touches)

....

....

....

This menu works well because:

❑ It always brings good comments

❑ Everything is fresh and seasonal

❑ Other reasons ....

❑ Quick to prepare

❑ Kids like it

❑ It's unusual

❑ Flavors are well balanced

❑ Free of last-minute stress

❑ Great party or celebration meal

This menu is especially good for:

❑ Thanksgiving ❑ Christmas

❑ Old friends ❑ New friends

❑ Other reasons ....

❑ Birthdays

❑ Easter

❑ Neighbors

❑ Sunday lunches

❑ Picnics

❑ Colleagues

❑ After the game

❑ Cooking Club

Food I've Served to Family and Friends

Date .... Time of Day ....

The Occasion ....

Guest List

....

....

....

....

Menu	Recipe Source (and page number)	Comments (about this dish)
....	....	....
....	....	....
....	....	....
....	....	....
....	....	....

Decorations (Centerpiece, colors, linens used, flowers, candles, other speical touches)

....

....

....

This menu works well because:
- ❑ Quick to prepare
- ❑ Flavors are well balanced
- ❑ It always brings good comments
- ❑ Kids like it
- ❑ Free of last-minute stress
- ❑ Everything is fresh and seasonal
- ❑ It's unusual
- ❑ Great party or celebration meal
- ❑ Other reasons ....

This menu is especially good for:
- ❑ Birthdays
- ❑ Sunday lunches
- ❑ After the game
- ❑ Thanksgiving
- ❑ Christmas
- ❑ Easter
- ❑ Picnics
- ❑ Cooking Club
- ❑ Old friends
- ❑ New friends
- ❑ Neighbors
- ❑ Colleagues
- ❑ Other reasons ....

Food I've Served to Family and Friends

Date .... Time of Day ....
The Occasion ....

Guest List

....
....
....
....

Menu	Recipe Source (and page number)	Comments (about this dish on this occasion)
....	....	....
....	....	....
....	....	....

Decorations (Centerpiece, colors, flowers, linens used, candles, other speical touches)

....
....
....
....

This menu works well because:
❑ It always brings good comments
❑ Everything is fresh and seasonal
❑ Other reasons ....

❑ Quick to prepare
❑ Kids like it
❑ It's unusual

❑ Flavors are well balanced
❑ Free of last-minute stress
❑ Great party or celebration meal

This menu is especially good for:
❑ Thanksgiving   ❑ Christmas
❑ Old friends   ❑ New friends
❑ Other reasons ....

❑ Birthdays
❑ Easter
❑ Neighbors

❑ Sunday lunches
❑ Picnics
❑ Colleagues

❑ After the game
❑ Cooking Club

Food I've Served to Family and Friends

Date .... Time of Day ....

The Occasion ....

Guest List

....

....

....

....

Menu	Recipe Source (and page number)	Comments (about this dish on this occasion)
....	....	....
....	....	....
....	....	....
....	....	....
....	....	....

Decorations (Centerpiece, colors, linens used, flowers, candles, other speical touches)

....

....

....

This menu works well because:
- ❏ It always brings good comments
- ❏ Everything is fresh and seasonal
- ❏ Quick to prepare
- ❏ Kids like it
- ❏ It's unusual
- ❏ Flavors are well balanced
- ❏ Free of last-minute stress
- ❏ Great party or celebration meal
- ❏ Other reasons ....

This menu is especially good for:
- ❏ Birthdays
- ❏ Sunday lunches
- ❏ After the game
- ❏ Thanksgiving
- ❏ Christmas
- ❏ Easter
- ❏ Picnics
- ❏ Cooking Club
- ❏ Old friends
- ❏ New friends
- ❏ Neighbors
- ❏ Colleagues
- ❏ Other reasons ....

Food I've Served to Family and Friends

Date .... Time of Day ....

The Occasion ....

Guest List

....

....

....

....

Menu	Recipe Source (and page number)	Comments (about this dish)
....	....	....
....	....	....
....	....	....
....	....	....
....	....	....

Decorations (Centerpiece, colors, linens used, flowers, candles, other speical touches)

....

....

....

This menu works well because:
❏ Quick to prepare   ❏ Flavors are well balanced
❏ It always brings good comments   ❏ Kids like it   ❏ Free of last-minute stress
❏ Everything is fresh and seasonal   ❏ It's unusual   ❏ Great party or celebration meal
❏ Other reasons ....

This menu is especially good for:
❏ Birthdays   ❏ Sunday lunches   ❏ After the game
❏ Thanksgiving   ❏ Christmas   ❏ Easter   ❏ Picnics   ❏ Cooking Club
❏ Old friends   ❏ New friends   ❏ Neighbors   ❏ Colleagues
❏ Other reasons ....

Food I've Served to Family and Friends

Date .... Time of Day ....

The Occasion ....

Guest List

....

....

....

....

Menu	Recipe Source (and page number)	Comments (about this dish)
....	....	....
....	....	....
....	....	....
....	....	....
....	....	....

Decorations (Centerpiece, colors, linens used, other speical touches)

....

....

....

This menu works well because:
- ❏ It always brings good comments
- ❏ Everything is fresh and seasonal
- ❏ Other reasons ....

- ❏ Quick to prepare
- ❏ Kids like it
- ❏ It's unusual

- ❏ Flavors are well balanced
- ❏ Free of last-minute stress
- ❏ Great party or celebration meal

This menu is especially good for:
- ❏ Thanksgiving   ❏ Christmas
- ❏ Old friends   ❏ New friends
- ❏ Other reasons ....

- ❏ Birthdays
- ❏ Easter
- ❏ Neighbors

- ❏ Sunday lunches
- ❏ Picnics
- ❏ Colleagues

- ❏ After the game
- ❏ Cooking Club

Food I've Served to Family and Friends

Date .... Time of Day ....

The Occasion ....

Guest List

....

....

....

....

Menu	Recipe Source (and page number)	Comments (about this dish on this occasion)
....	....	....
....	....	....
....	....	....
....	....	....
....	....	....

Decorations (Centerpiece, colors, linens used, flowers, candles, other speical touches)

....

....

....

This menu works well because: ❑ Quick to prepare   ❑ Flavors are well balanced

❑ It always brings good comments   ❑ Kids like it   ❑ Free of last-minute stress

❑ Everything is fresh and seasonal   ❑ It's unusual   ❑ Great party or celebration meal

❑ Other reasons ....

This menu is especially good for: ❑ Birthdays   ❑ Sunday lunches   ❑ After the game

❑ Thanksgiving   ❑ Christmas   ❑ Easter   ❑ Picnics   ❑ Cooking Club

❑ Old friends   ❑ New friends   ❑ Neighbors   ❑ Colleagues

❑ Other reasons ....

Food I've Served to Family and Friends

Date .... Time of Day ....

The Occasion ....

Guest List

....

....

....

....

Menu	Recipe Source (and page number)	Comments (about this dish on this occasion)
....	....	....
....	....	....
....	....	....

Decorations (Centerpiece, colors, flowers, linens used, candles, other speical touches)

....

....

....

....

This menu works well because:
- ❑ Quick to prepare
- ❑ Flavors are well balanced
- ❑ It always brings good comments
- ❑ Kids like it
- ❑ Free of last-minute stress
- ❑ Everything is fresh and seasonal
- ❑ It's unusual
- ❑ Great party or celebration meal
- ❑ Other reasons ....

This menu is especially good for:
- ❑ Birthdays
- ❑ Sunday lunches
- ❑ After the game
- ❑ Thanksgiving
- ❑ Christmas
- ❑ Easter
- ❑ Picnics
- ❑ Cooking Club
- ❑ Old friends
- ❑ New friends
- ❑ Neighbors
- ❑ Colleagues
- ❑ Other reasons ....

Food I've Served to Family and Friends

Date .... Time of Day ....

The Occasion ....

Guest List

....

....

....

....

Menu	Recipe Source (and page number)	Comments (about this dish)
....	....	....
....	....	....
....	....	....
....	....	....
....	....	....

Decorations (Centerpiece, colors, linens used, flowers, candles, other speical touches)

....

....

....

This menu works well because: ❏ Quick to prepare   ❏ Flavors are well balanced

❏ It always brings good comments   ❏ Kids like it   ❏ Free of last-minute stress

❏ Everything is fresh and seasonal   ❏ It's unusual   ❏ Great party or celebration meal

❏ Other reasons ....

This menu is especially good for: ❏ Birthdays   ❏ Sunday lunches   ❏ After the game

❏ Thanksgiving   ❏ Christmas   ❏ Easter   ❏ Picnics   ❏ Cooking Club

❏ Old friends   ❏ New friends   ❏ Neighbors   ❏ Colleagues

❏ Other reasons ....

Food I've Served to Family and Friends

Date .... Time of Day ....

The Occasion ....

Guest List

....

....

....

....

Menu	Recipe Source (and page number)	Comments (about this dish)
....	....	....
....	....	....
....	....	....
....	....	....
....	....	....

Decorations (Centerpiece, colors, linens used, flowers, candles, other speical touches)

....

....

....

This menu works well because:
- ❑ Quick to prepare
- ❑ Flavors are well balanced
- ❑ It always brings good comments
- ❑ Kids like it
- ❑ Free of last-minute stress
- ❑ Everything is fresh and seasonal
- ❑ It's unusual
- ❑ Great party or celebration meal
- ❑ Other reasons ....

This menu is especially good for:
- ❑ Birthdays
- ❑ Sunday lunches
- ❑ After the game
- ❑ Thanksgiving
- ❑ Christmas
- ❑ Easter
- ❑ Picnics
- ❑ Cooking Club
- ❑ Old friends
- ❑ New friends
- ❑ Neighbors
- ❑ Colleagues
- ❑ Other reasons ....

Food I've Served to Family and Friends

Date .... Time of Day ....

The Occasion ....

Guest List

....

....

....

....

Menu	Recipe Source (and page number)	Comments (about this dish on this occasion)
....	....	....
....	....	....
....	....	....

Decorations (Centerpiece, colors, flowers, linens used, candles, other speical touches)

....

....

....

....

This menu works well because:
- ❏ Quick to prepare
- ❏ Flavors are well balanced
- ❏ It always brings good comments
- ❏ Kids like it
- ❏ Free of last-minute stress
- ❏ Everything is fresh and seasonal
- ❏ It's unusual
- ❏ Great party or celebration meal
- ❏ Other reasons ....

This menu is especially good for:
- ❏ Birthdays
- ❏ Sunday lunches
- ❏ After the game
- ❏ Thanksgiving
- ❏ Christmas
- ❏ Easter
- ❏ Picnics
- ❏ Cooking Club
- ❏ Old friends
- ❏ New friends
- ❏ Neighbors
- ❏ Colleagues
- ❏ Other reasons ....

Food I've Served to Family and Friends

Date .... Time of Day ....

The Occasion ....

Guest List

....

....

....

....

Menu	Recipe Source (and page number)	Comments (about this dish on this occasion)
....	....	....
....	....	....
....	....	....
....	....	....
....	....	....

Decorations (Centerpiece, colors, linens used, flowers, candles, other speical touches)

....

....

....

This menu works well because:
- ❑ Quick to prepare
- ❑ Flavors are well balanced
- ❑ It always brings good comments
- ❑ Kids like it
- ❑ Free of last-minute stress
- ❑ Everything is fresh and seasonal
- ❑ It's unusual
- ❑ Great party or celebration meal
- ❑ Other reasons ....

This menu is especially good for:
- ❑ Birthdays
- ❑ Sunday lunches
- ❑ After the game
- ❑ Thanksgiving
- ❑ Christmas
- ❑ Easter
- ❑ Picnics
- ❑ Cooking Club
- ❑ Old friends
- ❑ New friends
- ❑ Neighbors
- ❑ Colleagues
- ❑ Other reasons ....

Food I've Served to Family and Friends

Date .... Time of Day ....

The Occasion ....

Guest List

....　　　　...

....　　　　...

....　　　　...

....　　　　...

Menu	Recipe Source (and page number)	Comments (about this dish on this occasion)
....	....	....
....	....	....
....	....	....

Give Thanks

Decorations (Centerpiece, colors, flowers, linens used, candles, other speical touches)

....

....

....

....

This menu works well because:

❑ It always brings good comments
❑ Everything is fresh and seasonal
❑ Other reasons ....

❑ Quick to prepare
❑ Kids like it
❑ It's unusual

❑ Flavors are well balanced
❑ Free of last-minute stress
❑ Great party or celebration meal

This menu is especially good for:

❑ Thanksgiving　❑ Christmas
❑ Old friends　❑ New friends
❑ Other reasons ....

❑ Birthdays
❑ Easter
❑ Neighbors

❑ Sunday lunches
❑ Picnics
❑ Colleagues

❑ After the game
❑ Cooking Club

Food I've Served to Family and Friends

Date .... Time of Day ....

The Occasion ....

Guest List

....
....
....
....

Menu	Recipe Source (and page number)	Comments (about this dish)
....	....	....
....	....	....
....	....	....
....	....	....

Decorations (Centerpiece, colors, linens used, other speical touches)

....
....
....

This menu works well because: ❑ Quick to prepare   ❑ Flavors are well balanced

❑ It always brings good comments   ❑ Kids like it   ❑ Free of last-minute stress

❑ Everything is fresh and seasonal   ❑ It's unusual   ❑ Great party or celebration meal

❑ Other reasons ....

This menu is especially good for: ❑ Birthdays   ❑ Sunday lunches   ❑ After the game

❑ Thanksgiving   ❑ Christmas   ❑ Easter   ❑ Picnics   ❑ Cooking Club

❑ Old friends   ❑ New friends   ❑ Neighbors   ❑ Colleagues

❑ Other reasons ....

Food I've Served to Family and Friends

Date .... Time of Day ....

The Occasion ....

Guest List

....

....

....

....

Menu	Recipe Source (and page number)	Comments (about this dish)
....	....	
....	....	
....	....	
....	....	
....	....	

Decorations (Centerpiece, colors, linens used, flowers, candles, other speical touches)

....

....

....

This menu works well because:
❑ Quick to prepare   ❑ Flavors are well balanced
❑ It always brings good comments   ❑ Kids like it   ❑ Free of last-minute stress
❑ Everything is fresh and seasonal   ❑ It's unusual   ❑ Great party or celebration meal
❑ Other reasons ....

This menu is especially good for:
❑ Birthdays   ❑ Sunday lunches   ❑ After the game
❑ Thanksgiving   ❑ Christmas   ❑ Easter   ❑ Picnics   ❑ Cooking Club
❑ Old friends   ❑ New friends   ❑ Neighbors   ❑ Colleagues
❑ Other reasons ....

Food I've Served to Family and Friends

Date .... Time of Day ....

The Occasion ....

Guest List

....

....

....

....

Menu	Recipe Source (and page number)	Comments (about this dish on this occasion)
....	....	....
....	....	....
....	....	....

Decorations (Centerpiece, colors, flowers, linens used, candles, other speical touches)

....

....

....

....

This menu works well because:

❑ It always brings good comments
❑ Everything is fresh and seasonal
❑ Other reasons ....

❑ Quick to prepare
❑ Kids like it
❑ It's unusual

❑ Flavors are well balanced
❑ Free of last-minute stress
❑ Great party or celebration meal

This menu is especially good for:

❑ Thanksgiving   ❑ Christmas
❑ Old friends   ❑ New friends
❑ Other reasons ....

❑ Birthdays
❑ Easter
❑ Neighbors

❑ Sunday lunches
❑ Picnics
❑ Colleagues

❑ After the game
❑ Cooking Club

Food I've Served to Family and Friends

Date .... Time of Day ....

The Occasion ....

Guest List

....

....

....

....

Menu	Recipe Source (and page number)	Comments (about this dish)
....	....	....
....	....	....
....	....	....
....	....	....
....	....	....

Decorations (Centerpiece, colors, linens used, flowers, candles, other speical touches)

....

....

....

This menu works well because:
- ❏ Quick to prepare
- ❏ Flavors are well balanced
- ❏ It always brings good comments
- ❏ Kids like it
- ❏ Free of last-minute stress
- ❏ Everything is fresh and seasonal
- ❏ It's unusual
- ❏ Great party or celebration meal
- ❏ Other reasons ....

This menu is especially good for:
- ❏ Birthdays
- ❏ Sunday lunches
- ❏ After the game
- ❏ Thanksgiving
- ❏ Christmas
- ❏ Easter
- ❏ Picnics
- ❏ Cooking Club
- ❏ Old friends
- ❏ New friends
- ❏ Neighbors
- ❏ Colleagues
- ❏ Other reasons ....

Food I've Served to Family and Friends

Date .... Time of Day ....

The Occasion ....

Guest List

....

....

....

....

Menu	Recipe Source (and page number)	Comments (about this dish on this occasion)
....	....	....
....	....	....
....	....	....

Decorations (Centerpiece, colors, flowers, linens used, candles, other speical touches)

....

....

....

....

This menu works well because:

❑ Quick to prepare   ❑ Flavors are well balanced

❑ It always brings good comments   ❑ Kids like it   ❑ Free of last-minute stress

❑ Everything is fresh and seasonal   ❑ It's unusual   ❑ Great party or celebration meal

❑ Other reasons ....

This menu is especially good for:

❑ Birthdays   ❑ Sunday lunches   ❑ After the game

❑ Thanksgiving   ❑ Christmas   ❑ Easter   ❑ Picnics   ❑ Cooking Club

❑ Old friends   ❑ New friends ❑ Neighbors   ❑ Colleagues

❑ Other reasons ....

Food I've Served to Family and Friends

Date .... Time of Day ....

The Occasion ....

Guest List

....
....
....
....

Menu	Recipe Source (and page number)	Comments (about this dish)
....	....	....
....	....	....
....	....	....
....	....	....
....	....	....

Decorations (Centerpiece, colors, linens used, flowers, candles, other speical touches)

....
....
....

This menu works well because:
- ❑ Quick to prepare
- ❑ Flavors are well balanced
- ❑ It always brings good comments
- ❑ Kids like it
- ❑ Free of last-minute stress
- ❑ Everything is fresh and seasonal
- ❑ It's unusual
- ❑ Great party or celebration meal
- ❑ Other reasons ....

This menu is especially good for:
- ❑ Birthdays
- ❑ Sunday lunches
- ❑ After the game
- ❑ Thanksgiving
- ❑ Christmas
- ❑ Easter
- ❑ Picnics
- ❑ Cooking Club
- ❑ Old friends
- ❑ New friends
- ❑ Neighbors
- ❑ Colleagues
- ❑ Other reasons ....

Food I've Served to Family and Friends

Date ....   Time of Day ....

The Occasion ....

Guest List

....

....

....

                       ....

Menu	Recipe Source (and page number)	Comments (about this dish)
....	....	....
....	....	....
....	....	....
....	....	....
....	....	....

Decorations (Centerpiece, colors, linens used, other speical touches)

....

....

....

This menu works well because:
- ❑ Quick to prepare   ❑ Flavors are well balanced
- ❑ It always brings good comments   ❑ Kids like it   ❑ Free of last-minute stress
- ❑ Everything is fresh and seasonal   ❑ It's unusual   ❑ Great party or celebration meal
- ❑ Other reasons ....

This menu is especially good for:
- ❑ Birthdays   ❑ Sunday lunches   ❑ After the game
- ❑ Thanksgiving   ❑ Christmas   ❑ Easter   ❑ Picnics   ❑ Cooking Club
- ❑ Old friends   ❑ New friends   ❑ Neighbors   ❑ Colleagues
- ❑ Other reasons ....

Food I've Served to Family and Friends

Date ....   Time of Day ....

The Occasion ....

Guest List

....

....

....

....

Menu	Recipe Source (and page number)	Comments (about this dish on this occasion)
....	....	....
....	....	....
....	....	....
....	....	....
....	....	....

Decorations (Centerpiece, colors, linens used, flowers, candles, other speical touches)

....

....

....

This menu works well because: ❑ Quick to prepare   ❑ Flavors are well balanced

❑ It always brings good comments   ❑ Kids like it   ❑ Free of last-minute stress

❑ Everything is fresh and seasonal   ❑ It's unusual   ❑ Great party or celebration meal

❑ Other reasons ....

This menu is especially good for: ❑ Birthdays   ❑ Sunday lunches   ❑ After the game

❑ Thanksgiving   ❑ Christmas   ❑ Easter   ❑ Picnics   ❑ Cooking Club

❑ Old friends   ❑ New friends   ❑ Neighbors   ❑ Colleagues

❑ Other reasons ....

121

Food I've Served to Family and Friends

Date .... Time of Day ....

The Occasion ....

Guest List

....

....

....

....

Menu	Recipe Source (and page number)	Comments (about this dish on this occasion)
....	....	....
....	....	....
....	....	....

Decorations (Centerpiece, colors, flowers, linens used, candles, other speical touches)

....

....

....

....

This menu works well because:
❑ Quick to prepare ❑ Flavors are well balanced
❑ It always brings good comments ❑ Kids like it ❑ Free of last-minute stress
❑ Everything is fresh and seasonal ❑ It's unusual ❑ Great party or celebration meal
❑ Other reasons ....

This menu is especially good for:
❑ Birthdays ❑ Sunday lunches ❑ After the game
❑ Thanksgiving ❑ Christmas ❑ Easter ❑ Picnics ❑ Cooking Club
❑ Old friends ❑ New friends ❑ Neighbors ❑ Colleagues
❑ Other reasons ....

Food I've Served to Family and Friends

Date .... Time of Day ....

The Occasion ....

Guest List

....
....
....
....

Menu	Recipe Source (and page number)	Comments (about this dish)
....	....	....
....	....	....
....	....	....
....	....	....
....	....	....

Decorations (Centerpiece, colors, linens used, flowers, candles, other speical touches)

....
....
....

This menu works well because:
- ❑ Quick to prepare
- ❑ Flavors are well balanced
- ❑ It always brings good comments
- ❑ Kids like it
- ❑ Free of last-minute stress
- ❑ Everything is fresh and seasonal
- ❑ It's unusual
- ❑ Great party or celebration meal
- ❑ Other reasons ....

This menu is especially good for:
- ❑ Birthdays
- ❑ Sunday lunches
- ❑ After the game
- ❑ Thanksgiving
- ❑ Christmas
- ❑ Easter
- ❑ Picnics
- ❑ Cooking Club
- ❑ Old friends
- ❑ New friends
- ❑ Neighbors
- ❑ Colleagues
- ❑ Other reasons ....

Food I've Served to Family and Friends

Date .... Time of Day ....

The Occasion ....

Guest List

....

....

....

....

Menu	Recipe Source (and page number)	Comments (about this dish)
....	....	....
....	....	....
....	....	....
....	....	....
....	....	....

Decorations (Centerpiece, colors, linens used, flowers, candles, other speical touches)

....

....

....

This menu works well because:

❑ Quick to prepare ❑ Flavors are well balanced

❑ It always brings good comments ❑ Kids like it ❑ Free of last-minute stress

❑ Everything is fresh and seasonal ❑ It's unusual ❑ Great party or celebration meal

❑ Other reasons ....

This menu is especially good for:

❑ Birthdays ❑ Sunday lunches ❑ After the game

❑ Thanksgiving ❑ Christmas ❑ Easter ❑ Picnics ❑ Cooking Club

❑ Old friends ❑ New friends ❑ Neighbors ❑ Colleagues

❑ Other reasons ....

Food I've Served to Family and Friends

Date .... Time of Day ....

The Occasion ....

Guest List

....
....
....
....

Menu	Recipe Source (and page number)	Comments (about this dish on this occasion)
....	....	....
....	....	....
....	....	....
....	....	....
....	....	....

Decorations (Centerpiece, colors, linens used, flowers, candles, other speical touches)

....
....
....

This menu works well because:
- ❑ It always brings good comments
- ❑ Everything is fresh and seasonal
- ❑ Other reasons ....

- ❑ Quick to prepare
- ❑ Kids like it
- ❑ It's unusual

- ❑ Flavors are well balanced
- ❑ Free of last-minute stress
- ❑ Great party or celebration meal

This menu is especially good for:
- ❑ Birthdays
- ❑ Thanksgiving ❑ Christmas ❑ Easter ❑ Picnics ❑ Cooking Club
- ❑ Old friends ❑ New friends ❑ Neighbors ❑ Colleagues
- ❑ Sunday lunches ❑ After the game
- ❑ Other reasons ....

Food I've Served to Family and Friends

Date .... Time of Day ....
The Occasion ....

Guest List

....
....
....
....

Menu   Recipe Source   Comments
                             (and page number)   (about this dish on this occasion)

....
....
....

Decorations (Centerpiece, colors, flowers,
linens used, candles, other speical touches)

....
....
....
....

This menu works well because: ❑ Quick to prepare   ❑ Flavors are well balanced

❑ It always brings good comments   ❑ Kids like it   ❑ Free of last-minute stress

❑ Everything is fresh and seasonal ❑ It's unusual   ❑ Great party or celebration meal

❑ Other reasons ....

This menu is especially good for: ❑ Birthdays   ❑ Sunday lunches   ❑ After the game

❑ Thanksgiving   ❑ Christmas   ❑ Easter   ❑ Picnics   ❑ Cooking Club

❑ Old friends   ❑ New friends   ❑ Neighbors   ❑ Colleagues

❑ Other reasons ....

Food I've Served to Family and Friends

Date .... Time of Day ....

The Occasion ....

Guest List

....

....

....

....

Menu	Recipe Source (and page number)	Comments (about this dish)
....	....	....
....	....	....
....	....	....
....	....	....
....	....	....

Decorations (Centerpiece, colors, linens used, flowers, candles, other speical touches)

....

....

....

This menu works well because: ❑ Quick to prepare ❑ Flavors are well balanced

❑ It always brings good comments ❑ Kids like it ❑ Free of last-minute stress

❑ Everything is fresh and seasonal ❑ It's unusual ❑ Great party or celebration meal

❑ Other reasons ....

This menu is especially good for: ❑ Birthdays ❑ Sunday lunches ❑ After the game

❑ Thanksgiving ❑ Christmas ❑ Easter ❑ Picnics ❑ Cooking Club

❑ Old friends ❑ New friends ❑ Neighbors ❑ Colleagues

❑ Other reasons ....

127

Food I've Served to Family and Friends

Date .... Time of Day ....

The Occasion ....

Guest List

....

....

....

....

Menu	Recipe Source (and page number)	Comments (about this dish on this occasion)
....	....	....
....	....	....
....	....	....

Decorations (Centerpiece, colors, flowers, linens used, candles, other speical touches)

....

....

....

....

This menu works well because:

❑ It always brings good comments

❑ Everything is fresh and seasonal

❑ Other reasons ....

❑ Quick to prepare

❑ Kids like it

❑ It's unusual

❑ Flavors are well balanced

❑ Free of last-minute stress

❑ Great party or celebration meal

This menu is especially good for:

❑ Thanksgiving   ❑ Christmas

❑ Old friends   ❑ New friends

❑ Birthdays   ❑ Sunday lunches   ❑ After the game

❑ Easter   ❑ Picnics   ❑ Cooking Club

❑ Neighbors   ❑ Colleagues

❑ Other reasons ....

128

Food I've Served to Family and Friends

Date .... Time of Day ....

The Occasion ....

Guest List

....

....

....

....

Menu	Recipe Source (and page number)	Comments (about this dish on this occasion)
....	....	....
....	....	....
....	....	....
....	....	....
....	....	....

Decorations (Centerpiece, colors, linens used, flowers, candles, other speical touches)

....

....

....

This menu works well because:
- ❑ It always brings good comments
- ❑ Everything is fresh and seasonal
- ❑ Other reasons ....

- ❑ Quick to prepare
- ❑ Kids like it
- ❑ It's unusual

- ❑ Flavors are well balanced
- ❑ Free of last-minute stress
- ❑ Great party or celebration meal

This menu is especially good for:
- ❑ Thanksgiving   ❑ Christmas
- ❑ Old friends   ❑ New friends
- ❑ Other reasons ....

- ❑ Birthdays
- ❑ Easter
- ❑ Neighbors

- ❑ Sunday lunches
- ❑ Picnics
- ❑ Colleagues

- ❑ After the game
- ❑ Cooking Club

Food I've Served to Family and Friends

Date .... Time of Day ....

The Occasion ....

Guest List

....

....

....

....

Menu	Recipe Source (and page number)	Comments (about this dish)
....	....	....
....	....	....
....	....	....
....	....	....
....	....	....

Decorations (Centerpiece, colors, linens used, flowers, candles, other speical touches)

....

....

....

This menu works well because: ❑ Quick to prepare   ❑ Flavors are well balanced

❑ It always brings good comments   ❑ Kids like it   ❑ Free of last-minute stress

❑ Everything is fresh and seasonal   ❑ It's unusual   ❑ Great party or celebration meal

❑ Other reasons ....

This menu is especially good for: ❑ Birthdays   ❑ Sunday lunches   ❑ After the game

❑ Thanksgiving   ❑ Christmas   ❑ Easter   ❑ Picnics   ❑ Cooking Club

❑ Old friends   ❑ New friends   ❑ Neighbors   ❑ Colleagues

❑ Other reasons ....

Food I've Served to Family and Friends

Date .... Time of Day ....

The Occasion ....

Guest List

....

....

....

....

Menu	Recipe Source (and page number)	Comments (about this dish on this occasion)
....	....	....
....	....	....
....	....	....

Decorations (Centerpiece, colors, flowers, linens used, candles, other speical touches)

....

....

....

....

This menu works well because:
- ❑ It always brings good comments
- ❑ Everything is fresh and seasonal
- ❑ Other reasons ....

- ❑ Quick to prepare
- ❑ Kids like it
- ❑ It's unusual

- ❑ Flavors are well balanced
- ❑ Free of last-minute stress
- ❑ Great party or celebration meal

This menu is especially good for:
- ❑ Thanksgiving   ❑ Christmas
- ❑ Old friends   ❑ New friends
- ❑ Other reasons ....

- ❑ Birthdays
- ❑ Easter
- ❑ Neighbors

- ❑ Sunday lunches
- ❑ Picnics
- ❑ Colleagues

- ❑ After the game
- ❑ Cooking Club

131

Food I've Served to Family and Friends

Date .... Time of Day ....
The Occasion ....

Guest List

....
....
....
....

Menu   Recipe Source   Comments
                         (and page number)   (about this dish)

....
....
....
....
....

Decorations (Centerpiece, colors, linens used, flowers, candles, other speical touches)

....
....
....

This menu works well because: ❑ Quick to prepare   ❑ Flavors are well balanced
❑ It always brings good comments   ❑ Kids like it   ❑ Free of last-minute stress
❑ Everything is fresh and seasonal ❑ It's unusual   ❑ Great party or celebration meal
❑ Other reasons ....

This menu is especially good for: ❑ Birthdays   ❑ Sunday lunches   ❑ After the game
❑ Thanksgiving   ❑ Christmas   ❑ Easter   ❑ Picnics   ❑ Cooking Club
❑ Old friends   ❑ New friends   ❑ Neighbors   ❑ Colleagues
❑ Other reasons ....

Food I've Served to Family and Friends

Date .... Time of Day ....

The Occasion ....

Guest List

....

....

....

....

Menu	Recipe Source (and page number)	Comments (about this dish)
....	....	....
....	....	....
....	....	....
....	....	....
....	....	....

Decorations (Centerpiece, colors, linens used, other speical touches)

....

....

....

This menu works well because: ❏ Quick to prepare   ❏ Flavors are well balanced

❏ It always brings good comments   ❏ Kids like it   ❏ Free of last-minute stress

❏ Everything is fresh and seasonal ❏ It's unusual   ❏ Great party or celebration meal

❏ Other reasons ....

This menu is especially good for: ❏ Birthdays   ❏ Sunday lunches   ❏ After the game

❏ Thanksgiving   ❏ Christmas   ❏ Easter   ❏ Picnics   ❏ Cooking Club

❏ Old friends   ❏ New friends ❏ Neighbors   ❏ Colleagues

❏ Other reasons ....

Food I've Served to Family and Friends

Date .... Time of Day ....

The Occasion ....

Guest List

....

....

....

....

Menu	Recipe Source (and page number)	Comments (about this dish)
....	....	....
....	....	....
....	....	....
....	....	....
....	....	....

Decorations (Centerpiece, colors, linens used, flowers, candles, other speical touches)

....

....

....

This menu works well because:
- ❑ Quick to prepare
- ❑ Flavors are well balanced
- ❑ It always brings good comments
- ❑ Kids like it
- ❑ Free of last-minute stress
- ❑ Everything is fresh and seasonal
- ❑ It's unusual
- ❑ Great party or celebration meal
- ❑ Other reasons ....

This menu is especially good for:
- ❑ Birthdays
- ❑ Sunday lunches
- ❑ After the game
- ❑ Thanksgiving
- ❑ Christmas
- ❑ Easter
- ❑ Picnics
- ❑ Cooking Club
- ❑ Old friends
- ❑ New friends
- ❑ Neighbors
- ❑ Colleagues
- ❑ Other reasons ....

Food I've Served to Family and Friends

Date .... Time of Day ....
The Occasion ....

Guest List

....
....
....
....

Menu	Recipe Source (and page number)	Comments (about this dish on this occasion)
....	....	....
....	....	....
....	....	....

Decorations (Centerpiece, colors, flowers, linens used, candles, other speical touches)

....
....
....
....

This menu works well because:
- ❑ It always brings good comments
- ❑ Everything is fresh and seasonal
- ❑ Quick to prepare
- ❑ Kids like it
- ❑ It's unusual
- ❑ Flavors are well balanced
- ❑ Free of last-minute stress
- ❑ Great party or celebration meal
- ❑ Other reasons ....

This menu is especially good for:
- ❑ Birthdays
- ❑ Sunday lunches
- ❑ After the game
- ❑ Thanksgiving ❑ Christmas
- ❑ Easter
- ❑ Picnics
- ❑ Cooking Club
- ❑ Old friends ❑ New friends
- ❑ Neighbors
- ❑ Colleagues
- ❑ Other reasons ....

Food I've Served to Family and Friends

Date .... Time of Day ....

The Occasion ....

Guest List

....

....

....

....

Menu	Recipe Source (and page number)	Comments (about this dish on this occasion)
....	....	....
....	....	....
....	....	....
....	....	....
....	....	....

Decorations (Centerpiece, colors, linens used, flowers, candles, other speical touches)

....

....

....

This menu works well because:
- ❑ It always brings good comments
- ❑ Everything is fresh and seasonal
- ❑ Other reasons ....
- ❑ Quick to prepare
- ❑ Kids like it
- ❑ It's unusual
- ❑ Flavors are well balanced
- ❑ Free of last-minute stress
- ❑ Great party or celebration meal

This menu is especially good for:
- ❑ Birthdays
- ❑ Thanksgiving ❑ Christmas
- ❑ Old friends ❑ New friends
- ❑ Other reasons ....
- ❑ Sunday lunches
- ❑ Easter
- ❑ Neighbors
- ❑ After the game
- ❑ Picnics
- ❑ Colleagues
- ❑ Cooking Club

Food I've Served to Family and Friends

Date ....   Time of Day ....

The Occasion ....

Guest List

....

....

....

....

Menu	Recipe Source (and page number)	Comments (about this dish)
....	....	....
....	....	....
....	....	....
....	....	....
....	....	....

Decorations (Centerpiece, colors, linens used, flowers, candles, other speical touches)

....

....

....

This menu works well because:
❏ Quick to prepare   ❏ Flavors are well balanced
❏ It always brings good comments   ❏ Kids like it   ❏ Free of last-minute stress
❏ Everything is fresh and seasonal   ❏ It's unusual   ❏ Great party or celebration meal
❏ Other reasons ....

This menu is especially good for: ❏ Birthdays   ❏ Sunday lunches   ❏ After the game
❏ Thanksgiving   ❏ Christmas   ❏ Easter   ❏ Picnics   ❏ Cooking Club
❏ Old friends   ❏ New friends   ❏ Neighbors   ❏ Colleagues
❏ Other reasons ....

Food I've Served to Family and Friends

Date .... Time of Day ....
The Occasion ....

Guest List

....
....
....
                                        ....

Menu	Recipe Source (and page number)	Comments (about this dish)
....	....	....
....	....	....
....	....	....
....	....	....
....	....	....

Decorations (Centerpiece, colors, linens used, other speical touches)
....
....
....

This menu works well because:
- ❏ Quick to prepare
- ❏ Flavors are well balanced
- ❏ It always brings good comments
- ❏ Kids like it
- ❏ Free of last-minute stress
- ❏ Everything is fresh and seasonal
- ❏ It's unusual
- ❏ Great party or celebration meal
- ❏ Other reasons ....

This menu is especially good for:
- ❏ Birthdays
- ❏ Sunday lunches
- ❏ After the game
- ❏ Thanksgiving
- ❏ Christmas
- ❏ Easter
- ❏ Picnics
- ❏ Cooking Club
- ❏ Old friends
- ❏ New friends
- ❏ Neighbors
- ❏ Colleagues
- ❏ Other reasons ....

Food I've Served to Family and Friends

Date ....   Time of Day ....

The Occasion ....

Guest List

....

....

....

....

Menu	Recipe Source (and page number)	Comments (about this dish on this occasion)
....	....	....
....	....	....
....	....	....
....	....	....
....	....	....

Decorations (Centerpiece, colors, linens used, flowers, candles, other speical touches)

....

....

....

This menu works well because:
- ❑ It always brings good comments
- ❑ Everything is fresh and seasonal
- ❑ Quick to prepare
- ❑ Kids like it
- ❑ It's unusual
- ❑ Flavors are well balanced
- ❑ Free of last-minute stress
- ❑ Great party or celebration meal
- ❑ Other reasons ....

This menu is especially good for:
- ❑ Thanksgiving
- ❑ Christmas
- ❑ Old friends
- ❑ New friends
- ❑ Birthdays
- ❑ Easter
- ❑ Neighbors
- ❑ Sunday lunches
- ❑ Picnics
- ❑ Colleagues
- ❑ After the game
- ❑ Cooking Club
- ❑ Other reasons ....

Food I've Served to Family and Friends

Date .... Time of Day ....

The Occasion ....

Guest List

....

....

....

....

Menu	Recipe Source (and page number)	Comments (about this dish on this occasion)
....	....	....
....	....	....
....	....	....

Decorations (Centerpiece, colors, flowers, linens used, candles, other speical touches)

....

....

....

....

This menu works well because:

☐ Quick to prepare   ☐ Flavors are well balanced

☐ It always brings good comments   ☐ Kids like it   ☐ Free of last-minute stress

☐ Everything is fresh and seasonal   ☐ It's unusual   ☐ Great party or celebration meal

☐ Other reasons ....

This menu is especially good for:

☐ Birthdays   ☐ Sunday lunches   ☐ After the game

☐ Thanksgiving   ☐ Christmas   ☐ Easter   ☐ Picnics   ☐ Cooking Club

☐ Old friends   ☐ New friends   ☐ Neighbors   ☐ Colleagues

☐ Other reasons ....

Food I've Served to Family and Friends

Date .... Time of Day ....
The Occasion ....

Guest List

....
....
....
....

Menu	Recipe Source (and page number)	Comments (about this dish)
....	....	....
....	....	....
....	....	....
....	....	....
....	....	....

Decorations (Centerpiece, colors, linens used, flowers, candles, other speical touches)

....
....
....

This menu works well because:
❑ It always brings good comments
❑ Everything is fresh and seasonal
❑ Other reasons ....

❑ Quick to prepare
❑ Kids like it
❑ It's unusual

❑ Flavors are well balanced
❑ Free of last-minute stress
❑ Great party or celebration meal

This menu is especially good for:
❑ Thanksgiving   ❑ Christmas
❑ Old friends   ❑ New friends
❑ Other reasons ....

❑ Birthdays
❑ Easter
❑ Neighbors

❑ Sunday lunches
❑ Picnics
❑ Colleagues

❑ After the game
❑ Cooking Club

Food I've Served to Family and Friends

Date .... Time of Day ....

The Occasion ....

Guest List

....

....

....

....

Menu	Recipe Source (and page number)	Comments (about this dish)
....	....	....
....	....	....
....	....	....
....	....	....
....	....	....

Decorations (Centerpiece, colors, linens used, flowers, candles, other speical touches)

....

....

....

This menu works well because: ❑ Quick to prepare   ❑ Flavors are well balanced

❑ It always brings good comments   ❑ Kids like it   ❑ Free of last-minute stress

❑ Everything is fresh and seasonal   ❑ It's unusual   ❑ Great party or celebration meal

❑ Other reasons ....

This menu is especially good for: ❑ Birthdays   ❑ Sunday lunches   ❑ After the game

❑ Thanksgiving   ❑ Christmas   ❑ Easter   ❑ Picnics   ❑ Cooking Club

❑ Old friends   ❑ New friends   ❑ Neighbors   ❑ Colleagues

❑ Other reasons ....

Food I've Served to Family and Friends

Date .... Time of Day ....

The Occasion ....

Guest List

....

....

....

....

Menu	Recipe Source (and page number)	Comments (about this dish on this occasion)
....	....	....
....	....	....
....	....	....

Decorations (Centerpiece, colors, flowers,
linens used, candles, other speical touches)

....

....

....

....

This menu works well because:
- ❏ Quick to prepare
- ❏ Flavors are well balanced
- ❏ It always brings good comments
- ❏ Kids like it
- ❏ Free of last-minute stress
- ❏ Everything is fresh and seasonal
- ❏ It's unusual
- ❏ Great party or celebration meal
- ❏ Other reasons ....

This menu is especially good for:
- ❏ Birthdays
- ❏ Sunday lunches
- ❏ After the game
- ❏ Thanksgiving
- ❏ Christmas
- ❏ Easter
- ❏ Picnics
- ❏ Cooking Club
- ❏ Old friends
- ❏ New friends
- ❏ Neighbors
- ❏ Colleagues
- ❏ Other reasons ....

143

Tips to Remember

Grandma and Mom and your fabulous-cook neighbor seem not be around when you need immediate cooking advice.

Here is space to write down those especially help-ful tips you've been told or read. Note them here—and you'll know exactly where to flip when you're trying to remember whether or not to cover the sweet potato-cranberry bake when you put it in the oven.

I've started off each page in this section with a few Tips I've picked up along the way. But you'll want to record the information you find essential in the kitchen.

You'll feel surrounded by cooking companions as you fill these pages. You'll no longer be cooking alone, so to speak!

Tips to Remember

→ Keep **nuts**, **coconut**, and *whole wheat flour* in airtight containers **in the freezer** in order to retain their freshness and flavor.

→ A teaspoon or two of **brown sugar** in **tomato dishes** enhances the **flavor** and helps to **smooth out the acid**.

→ If you mistakenly add **too much salt** to a dish you're preparing, **drop in a potato** and continue cooking. The potato will help to absorb the extra salt.

Tips to Remember

→ Try baking with **glass pans** and **metal pans** to see which you prefer.
You may have to lower the oven temperature by 25-50 degrees when
cooking in glass pans to prevent burning.

→ If you're making **muffins** or **cupcakes**, but you're not filling all the muffin cups,
put a scant ¼ **cup of water** in each empty cup. That will prevent your muffin
tin from warping in the oven heat.

→ Place **cooked hamburger** in a strainer and **rinse** it under hot water
to **eliminate extra fat**.

Tips to Remember

→ When you find a recipe that you love, **make a notation** in the cookbook that it is **a great recipe**.

→ **Use "half-sheet" commercial baking pans** to avoid burning cookies. They are a little heavier than regular cookie sheets. You can sometimes find them **at a big-box store**, and they are usually available **at restaurant supply stores**, as well.

→ **To save peeling time** when using fresh tomatoes, dip the **tomatoes into boiling water** until their skins begin to crack. Then the skins will peel off easily.

Tips to Remember

→ Slice raw **chicken breast** while it's still partly **frozen**. It's much **easier** to handle that way.

→ Check the bread recipe carefully before you begin preparing it to be sure that you **have enough yeast**. The small store-bought packets of yeast hold only 1-2 tsp., and **recipes often call for 1 Tbsp. of yeast**. You may find it useful to **buy yeast in bulk** and keep it in the freezer.

→ Don't salt meat or a roast as you're browning it. Instead, **add it** to taste **at the end of the browning**. The meat will stay more moist, since **salt draws out moisture**.

....

....

....

....

....

....

....

....

....

....

Tips to Remember

→ **Pricking potatoes** all over with a fork before baking, **prevents** the potato from **exploding**.

→ When sautéing or frying, turn a **metal colander** or strainer upside down over the skillet. This allows **steam to escape** and **keeps fat from spattering**.

→ Don't **measure ingredients** over the bowl in which you are mixing or baking the recipe, in case more than you need **comes tumbling out**.

Tips to Remember

→ Have one or two **"company specials"** you can make when friends show up unexpectedly.

→ Yams and sweet potatoes are <u>not</u> the same. Yams are much drier. Learn to recognize the difference. Likewise, there are **many varieties of apples**, from very tart to very sweet, firm texture to soft. **Experiment with different kinds** to discover your favorite for a recipe.

→ Buy dried **herbs and spices** in small amounts because they **lose their flavor** over time.

....

....

....

....

....

....

....

....

....

....

....

Tips to Remember

→ Soups which include **cream should never be boiled**. The cream will curdle.

→ Thirty minutes before **making gravy**, add flour to cold water in a jar with
a screw-top lid. Close the lid tightly, shake the flour-water mixture vigorously,
let it sit awhile, shake it again, let it sit awhile. Do this 3 or 4 times before
you are ready to add it to the boiling broth. **The lumps will disappear**
by the time you are ready to pour it into the hot broth to thicken it.

→ Remember to use **leftover cooked vegetables** from
your refrigerator when making **soup**.

Tips to Remember

→ Take cookies off the baking sheet **as soon as you've taken them out of the oven** so they don't continue to bake from the heat of the pan.

→ Want to make **cupcakes from regular cake batter**? Just fill paper-lined muffin cups ¾ full. **Bake at 375 degrees for 20-25 minutes**. After 20 minutes, test the middle of several cupcakes to see if they're finished. Continue baking if needed.

→ Use **light brown sugar** for a **caramel** flavor. Use **dark brown sugar** when you prefer a **molasses** flavor and color.

....

....

....

....

....

....

....

....

....

....

....

....

Tips to Remember

→ Never add fresh **kiwi** to a salad using gelatin. It **will "un-gell"** the whole thing!

→ Before **whipping heavy cream**, stick the **mixing bowl and beaters in the freezer** for 10 minutes or more. The cold utensils will speed up the whipping process.

→ Always **cut brownies with a plastic knife**. It prevents clumping and ragged edges.

→ To get the **best height** and **texture** when making **muffins**, remember that the batter should be lumpy and the ingredients just moistened uniformly. In other words, **don't over-stir the batter**.

....

....

....

....

....

....

....

....

....

....

....

....

Tips to Remember

→ When browning meats, **don't crowd the skillet** or cooking pan. If the pieces are too close to each other, they'll **steam** in each other's juices **rather than browning**.

→ If your recipe calls for **3 Tablespoons of fresh basil**, and you have only dried basil, use **1 Tablespoon of dried basil**. In other words, 1 portion of dried herbs can be substituted for 3 portions of fresh herbs. And vice versa.

→ **Do not add salt** to cold water in a cooking pan. Wait until the water boils. Otherwise, the **salt can pit the pan**.

....

....

....

....

....

....

....

....

....

....

....

....

The Cousins —
Two shelves of bestselling cookbooks!

National bestsellers. More than 8.5 million copies already sold!

⇨ *For slow cookers:*

Fix-It and Forget-It 5-ingredient Favorites	*Fix-It and Forget-It Cookbook*	*Fix-It and Forget-It Lightly*	*Fix-It and Forget-It Recipes for Entertaining*	*Fix-It and Forget-It Diabetic Cookbook*

⇨ *For stove-top and oven:*

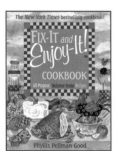   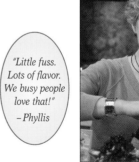

"Little fuss. Lots of flavor. We busy people love that!" – Phyllis

Fix-It and Enjoy-It! Cookbook	*Fix-It and Enjoy-It! Diabetic Cookbook*	*Fix-It and Enjoy-It! 5-Ingredient Recipes*

New York Times bestselling author
Phyllis Pellman Good